Desert Dance

Written by
Charlotte Armajo

Illustrated by
Teri Sloat

CELEBRATION PRESS
Pearson Learning Group

One warm September night,
when the desert sky was bright,

the animals started to prance and dance
under the harvest moon.

Lizard started to thump his tail,
thump his tail, thump his tail.

Lizard started to thump his tail
under the harvest moon.

Wild hares started to stamp their feet,
stamp their feet, stamp their feet.

Wild hares started to stamp their feet
under the harvest moon.

Rattlesnake started to shake his tail,
shake his tail, shake his tail.

8

Rattlesnake started to shake his tail
under the harvest moon.

Sage Hens started to flap their wings,
flap their wings, flap their wings.

10

Sage Hens started to flap their wings
under the harvest moon.

Wolves started to howl and prowl,
howl and prowl, howl and prowl.

Wolves started to howl and prowl
under the harvest moon.

Roadrunner started to jig and jog,
jig and jog, jig and jog.

Roadrunner started to jig and jog
under the harvest moon.

If you see the animals prance and dance,
prance and dance, prance and dance.
If you see the animals prance and dance,
look for the harvest moon.